# RESILIENT RESOLVE

Overcome Adversity, Maintain
Focus, Cultivate Grit and Build
Unstoppable Leadership

DILIP PATIL

## DEDICATION

This book is lovingly dedicated to my family—my unwavering foundation and guiding light. Your endless support and belief in me have fueled my journey of personal growth and have been the cornerstone in bringing this book to life. Your influence resonates in every word written and every lesson shared. Thank you for being my inspiration, my strength, and my home.

## YOUR GIFT: "THE SUCCESS FORMULA"

Thank you for joining me with **"Resilient Resolve."** As a token of appreciation, I'm excited to offer you a complimentary copy of my eBook, "The Success Formula." This guide has insights and strategies to propel you further on your path to success.

"The Success Formula" complements the principles explored in **"Resilient Resolve,"** providing actionable steps for achieving goals and enhancing one's life. To download your free copy, click the link below or scan the QR code:

This eBook is my way of saying thank you and supporting you in your journey toward success and happiness.

Best wishes,

Dilip Patil

# TABLE OF CONTENTS

# WELCOME TO THE
## "LEADERSHIP TRANSFORMED" SERIES

"Leadership is not about being in charge. It is about caring for those in your charge." – Simon Sinek.

Welcome to the transformative journey of leadership. In this series, we explore the depths of what it means to lead with resilience, compassion, and vision. Each book builds on the last, providing practical insights and inspiring stories to empower your leadership journey. Whether you are a seasoned leader or just beginning your path, the "Leadership Transformed" series is designed to help you navigate the complexities of modern leadership and emerge more robust, effective, and compassionate.

The "Leadership Transformed" series is more than a collection of books; it is a comprehensive guide to evolving as a leader in today's dynamic world. This series was created to address leaders' multifaceted challenges and provide actionable strategies to overcome them. Each book focuses on a critical aspect of leadership, offering deep insights into essential skills and traits defining influential leaders.

Our journey began with "Leadership Awakening," where we explored the foundational principles of leadership and how to awaken the leader within. From there, "Visionary Pathways" guided us through the importance of vision and strategic foresight in leadership. In "Masterful Communication," we delved into the art of effective communication, a cornerstone of successful leadership.

The series continued with "Decision Dynamics," which offered insights into making sound decisions under pressure. "Empathy & Empowerment" highlighted the power of leading with empathy and empowering those around you. Most recently, "Innovative Edge" focused on fostering innovation and staying ahead in an ever-changing landscape. Each book has contributed to a holistic understanding of leadership, preparing us for the crucial exploration of resilience in this seventh installment,

## Overview Of Previous Books

1. Leadership Awakening: This book introduced the foundational principles of leadership, helping readers discover their potential and understand the core values that drive effective leadership.

2. Visionary Pathways: This book focuses on the importance of having a clear vision and strategic foresight and provides tools for creating and communicating a compelling vision that inspires and guides teams.

3. Masterful Communication: This course emphasizes the critical role of communication in

leadership. It covers essential listening, speaking, and influencing skills, ensuring leaders can convey their messages effectively.

4. Decision Dynamics: Offered a deep dive into decision-making processes, helping leaders develop the skills to make informed and timely decisions, especially under pressure.

5. Empathy & Empowerment: Highlighted the importance of empathy in leadership and how empowering others can lead to a more engaged and motivated team.

6. Innovative Edge: Focused on fostering a culture of innovation within organizations, providing strategies for encouraging creativity and staying competitive in a rapidly changing environment.

In **"Resilient Resolve,"** we will delve into the vital trait of resilience and its leadership role. This book will equip you with the insights and tools to navigate adversity, maintain focus, and cultivate grit. You will learn to develop personal and emotional resilience, lead through crises, and foster a resilient team culture. Each chapter will provide practical advice, real-world examples, and exercises to help you integrate resilience into your leadership style.

- Strategies for building and maintaining personal resilience.
- Techniques for managing stress and maintaining well-being.
- Insights into leading effectively through crises and adversity.
- Tools for fostering a resilient team culture.
- Methods for learning from setbacks and failures.
- Approaches to sustaining high performance under pressure.
- Effective communication strategies during tough times.
- Guidance on planning for continuous resilience development.

As you embark on this new journey, remember that every step you take toward becoming a resilient leader transforms you and those around you. Resilience is not just about bouncing back from setbacks; it's about growing more robust and capable with each challenge you face. Let's dive into the heart of resilience and discover how it can reshape your leadership. We will explore the principles and practices to help you build an unstoppable leadership legacy. With gratitude,

Dilip Patil

# PREFACE

"Resilience is the ability to attack while running away." –
Wes Fessler.

The world of leadership is ever-changing, demanding a unique blend of strength, adaptability, and unwavering resolve. In this preface, I share my journey and the experiences that underscored the critical need for resilience in leadership. Reflecting on my path, the lessons learned, and the leaders who have inspired me, I am reminded of resilience's profound impact on effective leadership. I hope these insights will resonate with you and provide a solid foundation as we delve into this book's essence of resilient leadership.

My leadership journey began many years ago, driven by a passion for helping others reach their full potential and navigate the challenges of professional life. Over the years, I have encountered numerous obstacles and setbacks, each a valuable lesson in the importance of resilience. From the early days of my career, where uncertainty and rapid changes were the norms, to the present, where global crises and technological disruptions constantly reshape the landscape, resilience has been a constant companion.

Leading a team through a major organizational crisis was one of my most significant turning points. The experience was a baptism by fire, teaching me the necessity of staying calm, focused, and adaptable under pressure. During this time, I realized resilience was not just a trait but a skill that could be cultivated and strengthened.

Through these experiences, I have understood that resilient leaders can face adversity head-on, learn from their experiences, and emerge stronger. They are not immune to stress and setbacks but can bounce back and inspire their teams to do the same. This realization has profoundly influenced my approach to leadership and has been a driving force behind the creation of this book.

## THE NEED FOR RESILIENCE

In today's fast-paced and unpredictable world, the need for resilience in leadership is more critical than ever. Leaders are constantly confronted with challenges that test their limits—navigating economic downturns, managing organizational change, or responding to global crises. In such an environment, the ability to remain steadfast and adaptable is essential.

Resilience enables leaders to maintain focus and composure, even in the face of significant adversity. It allows them to turn challenges into opportunities, fostering a culture of continuous improvement and innovation within their organizations. Moreover, resilient leaders can inspire and support their teams, helping them to cope with stress and uncertainty and encouraging them to persevere.

This book, "Resilient Resolve," explores the various dimensions of resilience and provides practical strategies for developing this crucial trait. It is designed to help leaders at all levels build their resilience, lead through crises, and create resilient teams that can thrive. Through real-world examples, case studies, and actionable advice, you will gain the tools and insights needed to navigate the complexities of leadership with grace and tenacity.

Resilience is not a destination but a journey. As we move forward, let this book be your guide, helping you navigate the complexities of leadership with grace and tenacity. Each chapter is crafted to provide you with the knowledge and skills needed to build and sustain resilience in yourself and your team. We will explore the principles and practices to help you become a more resilient and effective leader. Embrace this journey, and let "Resilient Resolve" be your companion as you face the challenges and opportunities ahead with unwavering determination.

## YOUR GIFT: "THE SUCCESS FORMULA"

The Success Formula complements the principles explored in **"Resilient Resolve: Overcome Adversity, Maintain Focus, Cultivate Grit, and Build Unstoppable Leadership"** by providing actionable steps to achieve your goals and enhance your life.

To download your free copy, click the link below or scan the QR code:

This eBook is my way of saying thank you and supporting you in your journey toward success and happiness.

# INTRODUCTION

"The greatest glory in living lies not in never falling, but in rising every time we fall." – Nelson Mandela.

Resilience is the cornerstone of effective leadership. It enables leaders to navigate challenges, inspire their teams, and create lasting impact. In an era of constant change and unpredictability, resilience allows leaders to adapt, persevere, and thrive. This introduction sets the stage for exploring resilient leadership, providing the foundation for understanding its critical role and practical application in various leadership contexts.

Leaders face many challenges in today's rapidly evolving world—from economic fluctuations and technological advancements to organizational restructuring and unexpected crises. The ability to remain steadfast and practical in such adversity distinguishes exceptional leaders. Resilience is not just about enduring hardships; it's about leveraging these experiences to grow stronger and more capable.

Effective leadership is characterized by the capacity to bounce back from setbacks, learn from failures, and persist in pursuing goals despite obstacles. This dynamic quality of resilience enables leaders to maintain their focus and drive even when the path forward seems

14

uncertain. It also empowers leaders to foster a similar sense of resilience within their teams, creating an environment where challenges are viewed as opportunities for development and innovation.

This book, "Resilient Resolve: Overcome Adversity, Maintain Focus, Cultivate Grit, and Build Unstoppable Leadership," delves into the multifaceted nature of resilience. It provides insights into how leaders can develop and strengthen their resilience through practical strategies and real-world examples. By exploring the various dimensions of resilient leadership, this book aims to equip you with the tools and knowledge necessary to navigate the complexities of modern leadership effectively.

## IMPORTANCE OF RESILIENCE

Resilience is more than just the ability to bounce back from setbacks; it is about growing more substantial and more capable in the face of adversity. For leaders, resilience is essential for several reasons:

1. **Navigating Challenges:** Leaders often face unexpected challenges that require quick thinking and decisive action. Resilient leaders can remain calm and focused, making informed decisions under pressure. This ability to navigate challenges

effectively ensures the organization can weather storms and emerge stronger.

2. **Inspiring Teams:** A leader's response to adversity sets the tone for the entire team. Resilient leaders inspire confidence and motivation in their teams by demonstrating perseverance and a positive outlook. This inspiration is crucial for maintaining morale and productivity, especially during tough times.

3. **Creating Lasting Impact:** Resilient leaders can handle crises and leverage these experiences to drive long-term growth and success. They view setbacks as opportunities for learning and improvement, fostering a culture of continuous development and innovation within their organizations.

4. **Maintaining Focus:** In adversity, becoming distracted or overwhelmed is easy. Resilient leaders maintain their focus on the organization's goals and vision, ensuring that their teams stay aligned and motivated.

5. **Adapting to Change:** Rapid change and uncertainty characterize The modern business environment. Resilient leaders can adjust their strategies to meet new challenges and seize emerging opportunities.

## JOURNEY TO RESILIENT LEADERSHIP

The path to resilient leadership is a journey of growth and development. It involves embracing a mindset that views challenges as opportunities and continually seeking ways to build and strengthen resilience. Here are the critical stages in this journey:

- **Self-awareness:** The first step in becoming a resilient leader is self-awareness. This involves understanding your strengths and weaknesses, recognizing your stress triggers, and knowing how you respond to adversity. Self-awareness provides the foundation for personal growth and resilience.

- **Mindset Shift:** Developing a resilient mindset means shifting your perspective on challenges. Instead of viewing setbacks as failures, see them as opportunities for growth and learning. This positive outlook is essential for building resilience.

- **Skill Development:** Building resilience requires developing specific skills such as emotional regulation, stress management, and effective communication. These skills enable leaders to handle adversity with grace and composure.

- **Building Support Networks:** Resilient leaders understand the importance of support networks. They build strong relationships with mentors,

17

peers, and team members who can provide guidance, support, and encouragement during challenging times.

- **Learning from Experience:** Every challenge provides an opportunity to learn and grow. Resilient leaders reflect on their experiences, identify lessons learned, and apply these insights to future situations. This continuous learning process is critical to developing and maintaining resilience.

## OVERVIEW OF RESILIENCE

Resilience, in the context of leadership, encompasses several key elements:

- **Mental Toughness:** Staying focused and composed under pressure. Mental toughness involves maintaining a positive attitude, setting realistic goals, and staying committed to achieving them despite obstacles.
- **Emotional Regulation** is the capacity to manage and control emotions in stressful situations. Emotional regulation helps leaders maintain their composure and make rational decisions, even when faced with significant challenges.

- **Adaptability:** The willingness and ability to adjust to new circumstances and changing environments. Adaptable leaders are flexible and open to new ideas, allowing them to navigate uncertainty effectively.

- **Growth Mindset:** The belief that abilities and intelligence can be developed through effort and learning. Leaders with a growth mindset view challenges as opportunities to improve and grow rather than insurmountable obstacles.

- **Social Support:** Building and maintaining solid relationships with colleagues, mentors, and team members. Social support provides a network of resources and encouragement that helps leaders cope with stress and adversity.

- **Persistence:** The determination to keep going despite difficulties and setbacks. Persistent leaders do not give up easily; they stay committed to their goals and strive for success despite significant challenges.

This book will explore these elements in depth, providing practical strategies and real-life examples to help you develop and apply resilience in your leadership journey.

Understanding the essence of resilience is the first step. As we delve deeper into this book, you'll discover practical strategies and real-life examples to help you become a resilient leader. Each chapter is designed to provide you with the tools and insights needed to build and sustain resilience, enabling you to navigate the complexities of leadership with grace and tenacity. Let's embark on this journey together, transforming challenges into growth and success opportunities.

# 1  DEFINING RESILIENCE

"Success is not final, failure is not fatal: It is the courage to continue that count." – Winston Churchill.

What does it mean to be a resilient leader? This chapter defines resilience in the context of leadership, exploring its impact and sharing stories of leaders who embody this vital trait. Resilience is more than just bouncing back from setbacks; it is the ability to grow stronger and more capable through adversity. As we delve into the nuances of leadership resilience, we'll uncover how it shapes effective leadership and drives personal and organizational success.

Resilience is often perceived as the simple act of recovering from difficulties, but in leadership, it encompasses much more. A resilient leader withstands challenges and uses these experiences to boost personal growth and organizational improvement. This transformative quality allows leaders to navigate the complexities of their roles with fortitude and flexibility, fostering an environment where innovation and progress can thrive even in the face of obstacles.

The essence of resilience in leadership lies in the capacity to maintain focus, energy, and optimism despite setbacks. It involves a combination of emotional strength, mental agility, and a proactive mindset. Resilient leaders possess the courage to confront failures head-on, analyze their experiences, and implement changes that lead to better outcomes. This process of learning and adaptation is crucial for long-term success and sustainability in any organization.

Throughout history, numerous leaders have exemplified resilience, demonstrating how adversity can be an influential teacher and motivator. Their stories serve as compelling illustrations of how resilience can transform ordinary leadership into extraordinary influence. These leaders have faced significant challenges, from economic crises and political upheavals to personal hardships. Yet, they emerged more substantial and more effective, leaving a lasting impact on their organizations and communities.

For instance, consider the story of Nelson Mandela, who endured 27 years of imprisonment yet emerged as a symbol of hope and resilience, leading South Africa through a peaceful transition from apartheid. His ability to forgive, inspire, and lead with unwavering conviction exemplifies the power of resilience in leadership. Similarly, the journey of Steve Jobs, who was ousted from Apple, the company he co-founded, only to return years later and revolutionize the technology industry, highlights how resilience can drive innovation and success.

As we explore the concept of resilience in leadership, we will delve into the traits and behaviors that characterize resilient leaders. These include adaptability, emotional intelligence, perseverance, and a growth mindset. We will also examine practical strategies for developing and strengthening these traits, providing you with actionable insights to enhance your resilience.

Moreover, we will discuss the impact of resilience on organizational culture and performance. Resilient leaders create a ripple effect, fostering a resilient workforce better equipped to handle challenges, embrace change, and pursue continuous improvement. This positive organizational culture enhances employee well-being and engagement and drives sustained success and competitive advantage.

In this chapter, you will understand what it means to be a resilient leader. You will learn how to harness the power of resilience to navigate the inevitable challenges of leadership, inspire your team, and achieve remarkable results. By embracing resilience as a core aspect of your leadership approach, you will be well-prepared to turn adversity into opportunity and lead with confidence, clarity, and unwavering resolve.

## 1.1 LEADERSHIP RESILIENCE

Leadership resilience is the capacity of leaders to endure and thrive amidst challenges, uncertainties, and crises. It involves a combination of mental toughness, emotional regulation, adaptability, and a growth mindset. Let's break down these components:

1. **Mental Toughness:** Staying focused and composed under pressure. Mentally tough leaders maintain their cool in stressful situations, making clear-headed decisions and confidently leading their teams. They can classify stress and prioritize tasks effectively, ensuring they can handle multiple demands without losing sight of their goals.

2. **Emotional Regulation:** Resilient leaders are adept at managing their emotions and the emotions of those around them. They can remain calm and steady even when faced with intense pressure or unexpected setbacks. This emotional stability allows them to build trust and morale within their teams, fostering an environment where people feel supported and motivated.

3. **Adaptability:** Resilient leadership is characterized by adapting to changing circumstances. Adaptable leaders are open to new ideas, flexible, and can pivot strategies when

necessary. They see change as an opportunity rather than a threat and encourage their teams to embrace innovation and continuous improvement.

4. **Growth Mindset:** Leaders with a growth mindset believe that abilities and intelligence can be developed through dedication and hard work. They view challenges as opportunities for learning and growth rather than insurmountable obstacles. This mindset fosters resilience by encouraging a proactive and positive approach to overcoming difficulties.

By integrating these elements, resilient leaders create a foundation for sustainable success for themselves and their organizations. They can withstand the pressures of leadership and inspire their teams to rise to the occasion and achieve collective goals.

## 1.2 RESILIENCE IMPACT

The impact of resilience on leadership is profound and multifaceted. Here are some key areas where resilience makes a significant difference:

1. **Personal Well-being:** Resilient leaders are better equipped to handle stress and maintain well-being. They practice self-care, set

boundaries, and seek support when needed. This enhances their performance and sets a positive example for their teams.

2. **Team Dynamics:** A resilient leader fosters a resilient team. By demonstrating resilience, leaders instill confidence and stability within their teams. This creates a supportive and cohesive team environment where members feel empowered to take risks, learn from failures, and persist in facing challenges.

3. **Organizational Performance:** Resilient organizations are more agile and better able to adapt to changing market conditions. Leaders who prioritize resilience build cultures that encourage innovation, continuous learning, and strategic risk-taking. This adaptability enables organizations to stay competitive and thrive in dynamic environments.

4. **Crisis Management:** Resilient leaders provide the steady hand needed to navigate uncertainty during crises. They can quickly assess situations, make informed decisions, and communicate effectively with stakeholders. Their ability to remain calm and focused under pressure helps minimize the impact of crises and accelerate recovery.

5. **Long-term Success:** Resilience contributes to long-term success by fostering a culture of perseverance and continuous improvement. Leaders who prioritize resilience are committed to ongoing personal and professional development for themselves and their teams. This commitment to growth ensures that the organization remains strong and capable of overcoming future challenges.

## 1.3 LEADER STORIES

To illustrate the concept of leadership resilience, let's explore stories of leaders who have demonstrated exceptional resilience:

1. **Nelson Mandela:** Mandela's journey is a powerful example of resilience in adversity. Despite spending 27 years in prison, he emerged with a vision of reconciliation and led South Africa through a peaceful transition from apartheid to democracy. Mandela's ability to maintain focus, hope, and dedication to his principles exemplifies true leadership resilience.

2. **Angela Merkel:** As the Chancellor of Germany, Angela Merkel has navigated numerous crises, including the Eurozone debt crisis, the refugee crisis, and the COVID-19 pandemic. Her calm

demeanor, pragmatic decision-making, and ability to adapt to evolving situations have been crucial to her leadership success. Merkel's resilience has stabilized Germany and positioned it as a leader in the European Union.

3. **Howard Schultz:** The former CEO of Starbucks, Howard Schultz, faced significant challenges in his career, including the company's near collapse in 2008. Schultz's resilience was evident in his decision to return as CEO and implement a comprehensive turnaround strategy. By focusing on the company's core values and adapting to market changes, he revitalized Starbucks and set it on a path of sustained growth.

4. **Malala Yousafzai:** Malala's story is a testament to the power of resilience. After surviving an assassination attempt by the Taliban, she continued to advocate for girls' education, becoming a global symbol of courage and determination. Despite the immense risks and challenges, Malala's unwavering commitment to her cause highlights the profound impact of resilient leadership.

These stories demonstrate that resilience is not limited to any specific context or role. It is a universal trait that enables leaders to overcome adversity, inspire others, and create lasting positive change.

Defining resilience is just the beginning. As we continue, we'll explore how to build and sustain this essential quality in your leadership journey. By understanding resilience's key components and impact, you will be better equipped to navigate challenges and lead confidently and gracefully. The chapters ahead will provide practical strategies and real-life examples to help you develop and integrate resilience into your leadership practice, transforming obstacles into opportunities for growth and success.

# 2  PERSONAL RESILIENCE

"The oak fought the wind and was broken; the willow bent when it must and survived." – Robert Jordan.

Personal resilience is the foundation upon which all other aspects of resilient leadership are built. It enables leaders to maintain their equilibrium and effectiveness in adversity. Unlike the rigid oak that breaks under pressure, resilient leaders, like the flexible willow, adapt to their circumstances and emerge stronger. This chapter provides strategies for building personal resilience, managing stress, and cultivating a resilient mindset. Leaders can better navigate challenges and inspire team resilience by developing these core skills.

In the ever-evolving leadership landscape, personal resilience is the bedrock that supports and sustains all other leadership qualities. The inner strength allows leaders to stay grounded amidst chaos, recover from setbacks swiftly, and continue moving forward with purpose and determination. As we explore the components of personal resilience, you'll discover practical tools and techniques that can transform your approach to leadership.

This chapter will guide you through building personal resilience by offering concrete strategies for self-care, goal-setting, and continuous learning. You'll learn how to effectively manage stress through time-tested methods like mindfulness, relaxation techniques, and exercise. Additionally, we will delve into the importance of maintaining a resilient mindset—a crucial aspect that encompasses a growth-oriented outlook, optimism, self-compassion, problem-solving skills, and emotional regulation.

Mastering these elements will enhance your resilience and set a powerful example for your team. A resilient leader is a source of inspiration and stability, someone who can guide their team through the most demanding challenges and emerge with renewed strength and clarity. As you implement these strategies, you'll find that resilience is a trait you possess and a skill you can develop and refine over time.

With a solid foundation of personal resilience, you will be better equipped to lead effectively, navigate leadership's inevitable ups and downs, and inspire those around you to cultivate their resilience. Let's embark on this journey together, starting with the core principles and practices that build personal resilience and pave the way for resilient leadership.

## 2.1 BUILDING STRATEGIES

Building personal resilience involves developing habits and practices that enhance your ability to cope with and recover from stress. Here are some effective strategies:

1. **Self-Care:** Prioritize physical, mental, and emotional well-being. Regular exercise, a balanced diet, adequate sleep, and mindfulness practices such as meditation or yoga are essential for maintaining resilience. These activities help to reduce stress, increase energy levels, and improve overall health, making you more resilient to life's challenges.

2. **Goal Setting:** Set realistic and achievable goals. Break larger objectives into smaller, manageable tasks. This approach makes goals more attainable and provides a sense of accomplishment and progress, boosting resilience.

3. **Positive Relationships:** Build and maintain a strong support network. Surround yourself with positive and supportive people who can offer encouragement, advice, and companionship. A network of trusted individuals provides emotional support and practical assistance during difficult times.

4. **Continuous Learning:** Embrace a lifelong learning mindset. Seek opportunities for personal

and professional development through courses, workshops, reading, and networking. Continuous learning helps to keep your mind agile and open to new ideas, enhancing your adaptability and resilience.

5. **Reflective Practice:** Regularly reflect on your experiences, challenges, and successes. Journaling or talking with a mentor can provide valuable insights and help you understand your responses to stress. Reflection allows you to learn from your experiences and develop strategies for future challenges.

## 2.2 STRESS MANAGEMENT

Effectively managing stress is crucial for maintaining personal resilience. Here are some techniques to help you manage stress:

1. **Time Management:** Prioritize tasks and manage your time effectively. Use calendars, to-do lists, and time-blocking to organize your day and reduce overwhelming feelings. Prioritizing your workload ensures you focus on the most important and avoid unnecessary stress.

2. **Relaxation Techniques:** Practice relaxation techniques such as deep breathing, progressive muscle relaxation, or visualization. These

techniques can help reduce physical and mental tension, promoting a state of calm and relaxation.

3. **Mindfulness:** Incorporate mindfulness practices into your daily routine. Mindfulness involves being present in the moment and aware of your thoughts and feelings without judgment. Regular mindfulness can reduce stress, improve focus, and enhance emotional regulation.

4. **Exercise:** Engage in regular physical activity. Exercise is a powerful stress reliever that boosts endorphins, improves mood, and enhances physical health. Find activities you enjoy, whether running, swimming, dancing, or yoga, and make them a regular part of your routine.

5. **Healthy Boundaries:** Establish healthy boundaries between work and personal life. Learn to say no to additional commitments that may cause undue stress. Prioritize self-care and personal time to recharge and maintain balance.

## 2.3 RESILIENT MINDSET

Cultivating a resilient mindset is about developing a positive and proactive approach to challenges. Here are the critical components of a resilient mindset:

1. **Growth Mindset:** Embrace the belief that abilities and intelligence can be developed

through effort and learning. View challenges as opportunities to grow and improve rather than insurmountable obstacles. This mindset encourages persistence and resilience in the face of setbacks.

2. **Optimism:** Maintain a positive outlook, even during difficult times. Focus on what you can control and look for the silver lining in challenging situations. Optimism helps to build resilience by fostering hope and motivation.

3. **Self-Compassion:** Practice self-compassion by treating yourself with kindness and understanding, especially during failure or difficulty. Recognize that setbacks are a normal part of life and an opportunity for growth. Self-compassion helps to build emotional resilience and reduce self-criticism.

4. **Problem-Solving Skills:** Develop practical problem-solving skills to tackle challenges head-on. Break problems into manageable parts, identify potential solutions, and take decisive action. Being proactive in addressing issues builds confidence and resilience.

5. **Emotional Regulation:** Learn to manage and regulate your emotions effectively. Techniques such as cognitive reappraisal (changing how you

think about a situation) and emotional expression (talking about your feelings) can help you maintain emotional balance and resilience.

Strengthening your resilience is a continuous process. By adopting these strategies, you'll be better equipped to handle whatever challenges come your way. Personal resilience forms the bedrock of effective leadership, enabling you to lead with confidence, composure, and strength. As we continue our exploration, we will build upon this foundation to develop the skills necessary for leading through crises and fostering resilience in others.

# 3 CRISIS LEADERSHIP

"Anyone can hold the helm when the sea is calm." –
Publilius Syrus.

Leading in times of crisis is an actual test of resilience. Crises are inevitable, whether they stem from economic downturns, natural disasters, or internal organizational disruptions. Such events can strike without warning, throwing even the most well-prepared organizations into turmoil. Crises' unpredictability and high stakes challenge leaders to demonstrate their true mettle. How leaders respond to these challenges can determine the fate of their teams and organizations.

In the face of adversity, a leader's ability to remain calm, make decisive decisions, and communicate effectively becomes paramount. Crises create high-pressure environments where emotions run high, and the margin for error is slim. Leaders must navigate through the chaos, providing direction and stability while ensuring the safety and well-being of their teams.

This chapter explores effective crisis navigation, decision-making under pressure, and real-world case studies. By understanding and mastering these aspects, you will be equipped to steer your organization through turbulent times with confidence and poise. We will delve into strategies for preparing for crises, maintaining clarity amidst confusion, and leading with strength and empathy.

Navigating a crisis requires a blend of foresight and adaptability. Leaders must anticipate potential challenges and develop contingency plans but must also be ready to pivot and adjust as the situation evolves. Effective crisis leadership involves balancing immediate, tactical responses with a long-term, strategic vision. This dual focus ensures leaders can address urgent needs while keeping sight of overarching goals.

Decision-making under pressure is another critical skill for crisis leaders. In high-stakes situations, quickly gathering information, evaluating options, and taking decisive action can distinguish between success and failure. Leaders must trust their instincts while leveraging their teams' collective intelligence. Collaborative decision-making can yield innovative solutions and build team cohesion, even in the most trying times.

To illustrate these principles, we will examine real-world case studies of leaders who have successfully navigated crises. These examples will highlight best practices and common pitfalls, offering valuable lessons that can be applied to your leadership journey. By learning from these experiences, you can develop the resilience and skills to lead through any storm.

As we explore these topics, remember that crisis leadership is not about having all the answers. It's about staying grounded, remaining flexible, and guiding your team with unwavering resolve. The insights and strategies in this chapter will empower you to face crises head-on, transforming challenges into opportunities for growth and strengthening your leadership capabilities.

With this foundation, you are prepared to dive deeper into the nuances of crisis leadership, learning how to navigate, decide, and lead through uncertainty. We will uncover the tools and mindset necessary to become a resilient and influential leader.

## 3.1 CRISIS NAVIGATION

Navigating a crisis requires a clear strategy and the ability to remain calm under pressure. Effective crisis navigation involves several key components:

1. **Preparation and Planning:** The best way to handle a crisis is to be prepared for it. This involves identifying potential risks and developing contingency plans. Regularly conduct crisis simulations and training sessions with your team to ensure everyone knows their roles and

responsibilities. A well-prepared team can respond more effectively and efficiently when a crisis occurs.

2. **Clear and transparent communication**: It is crucial during a crisis. Keep your team informed about the situation, your response plan, and any changes as they occur. Consistent communication helps reduce uncertainty and anxiety, keeping everyone aligned and focused on their tasks.

3. **Staying Calm:** As a leader, your demeanor sets the tone for your team. Staying calm and composed under pressure helps to reassure your team and maintain their confidence. Practice stress management techniques, such as deep breathing, mindfulness, and taking regular breaks, to help you remain calm.

4. **Prioritization:** In a crisis, it's important to prioritize tasks and resources effectively. Focus on the most critical issues first and allocate resources accordingly. Use a decision matrix or other prioritization tools to help you determine which tasks require immediate attention and which can be deferred.

5. **Flexibility**: Crises are unpredictable, and your initial plan may need to be adjusted as new information becomes available. Be flexible and

willing to pivot your strategy as needed. Encourage your team to remain adaptable and open to change.

## 3.2 DECISION MAKING

Making decisions under pressure is a critical skill for leaders during a crisis. Here are some strategies to enhance your decision-making capabilities:

1. **Gather Information:** Accurate and up-to-date information is essential in a crisis. Use reliable sources and verify facts before making decisions. Encourage your team to provide input and share their insights to understand the situation comprehensively.

2. **Assess the Situation:** Take a step back and assess the situation from multiple perspectives. Consider the short-term and long-term implications of potential decisions. Use SWOT analysis (Strengths, Weaknesses, Opportunities, Threats) to evaluate your options.

3. **Trust Your Instincts:** While relying on data and analysis is essential, don't ignore your instincts. Experienced leaders develop a sense of intuition that can guide them in making quick, effective decisions. Trust your gut feelings, especially when time is of the essence.

4. **Involve Your Team:** Collaborate with your team in decision-making. Diverse perspectives can lead to more innovative solutions. Encourage open discussions and listen to your team's ideas and concerns. This collaborative approach fosters a sense of ownership and commitment.

5. **Decisive Action:** Once you've gathered information and evaluated your options, take decisive action. Indecision can exacerbate a crisis and create additional stress for your team. Communicate your decisions and their rationale to ensure everyone understands the direction and roles.

## 3.3 CASE STUDIES

Learning from real-world examples can provide valuable insights into effective crisis leadership. Here are three case studies that illustrate different aspects of crisis management:

1. **Johnson & Johnson Tylenol Crisis (1982):** When cyanide-laced Tylenol capsules caused several deaths, Johnson & Johnson faced a significant crisis. The company's response is considered a textbook example of effective crisis management. They quickly recalled all Tylenol products, prioritized consumer safety, and

communicated transparently with the public. Their actions restored trust and ultimately strengthened their brand.

2. **Starbucks' Response to Racial Bias Incident (2018):** After two black men were arrested in a Philadelphia Starbucks, the company faced widespread criticism. CEO Kevin Johnson quickly apologized, met with the affected individuals, and closed over 8,000 stores for racial bias training. This decisive and transparent response helped to address the issue and demonstrate the company's commitment to diversity and inclusion.

3. **Airbnb's COVID-19 Response (2020):** The COVID-19 pandemic severely impacted the travel industry, and Airbnb was no exception. CEO Brian Chesky navigated the crisis by making difficult decisions, including laying off 25% of the workforce. However, the company prioritized supporting employees through generous severance packages and maintaining health benefits. Chesky also focused on communicating transparently with stakeholders and adapting the business model to include longer-term stays. This approach helped Airbnb survive the crisis and eventually go public.

These case studies highlight the importance of quick, decisive action, clear communication, and a focus on stakeholder needs in managing a crisis. You can apply similar principles to your leadership practice by learning from these examples.

Crisis leadership requires calm, clarity, and decisive action. The lessons from this chapter will prepare you to lead confidently through any storm. By mastering crisis navigation, enhancing your decision-making skills, and learning from real-world examples, you will be better equipped to steer your organization through turbulent times. The next chapter will delve into emotional resilience and intelligence as we continue our journey through resilience, providing further tools to strengthen our leadership capabilities.

# 4 EMOTIONAL RESILIENCE

"Life doesn't get easier or more forgiving, we get stronger and more resilient." – Steve Maraboli.

Emotional resilience is critical for maintaining balance and empathy as a leader. In the face of adversity, leaders with solid emotional resilience can navigate the complexities of human emotions—their own and those of their team members. This chapter covers emotional management techniques and empathy's role in leadership. By developing emotional resilience, leaders can build stronger connections with their teams, foster a supportive work environment, and maintain stability during turbulent times.

The modern leadership landscape is fraught with challenges that test a leader's strategic and operational capabilities and emotional fortitude. Emotional resilience allows leaders to remain grounded, composed, and practical, even when faced with significant stress or unexpected setbacks. The ability to recover quickly from emotional setbacks, adapt to change, and maintain a positive outlook is vital for leading teams through periods of uncertainty and change.

Emotional resilience begins with self-awareness and self-regulation. Leaders must first understand their emotional triggers and responses to manage them effectively. This self-knowledge enables leaders to maintain their composure, make rational decisions, and provide clear direction even in high-pressure situations. Emotional self-regulation prevents negative emotions from spilling into professional interactions, ensuring leaders can communicate effectively and maintain healthy relationships with their team members.

In addition to managing their own emotions, resilient leaders must also be attuned to the emotions of their team members. This is where empathy plays a crucial role. Empathy allows leaders to understand and share the feelings of others, creating a supportive and inclusive work environment. When leaders demonstrate empathy, they build trust and rapport, which is essential for team cohesion and morale. Empathetic leaders are better equipped to address the emotional needs of their team, providing the necessary support to help them navigate challenges and remain engaged and motivated.

Furthermore, emotional resilience helps leaders foster a culture of psychological safety within their organizations. When team members feel safe expressing their thoughts and emotions without fear of judgment or retribution, they are more likely to take risks, innovate, and collaborate effectively. This supportive environment encourages open communication, mutual respect, and collective problem-solving, all contributing to a resilient and high-performing team.

This chapter will explore practical techniques for building and enhancing emotional resilience. These techniques include mindfulness practices, stress management strategies, and cultivating a resilient mindset. We will also delve into the critical role of empathy in leadership and how to integrate empathetic practices into your daily interactions with your team. By mastering these skills, you can lead with strength and compassion, guiding your team through the highs and lows of organizational life with grace and resilience.

Emotional resilience is not a fixed trait but a dynamic capacity that can be developed and strengthened over time. As you engage with the concepts and practices outlined in this chapter, you will build the emotional resilience needed to handle leadership demands and create a positive and resilient organizational culture. Embrace the journey of developing emotional resilience, and you will find that it enhances your leadership effectiveness and overall well-being and fulfillment.

## 4.1 EMOTIONAL BALANCE

Emotional balance refers to maintaining stability and composure, even in stressful situations. Leaders who achieve emotional balance are better equipped to make rational decisions and lead effectively. Here are key strategies for maintaining emotional balance:

1. **Self-awareness:** Cultivate self-awareness by regularly reflecting on your emotions and how they influence your thoughts and behaviors. Practice mindfulness to become more attuned to your emotional state and recognize early signs of stress or imbalance.

2. **Mindfulness Practices:** Incorporate mindfulness practices such as meditation, deep breathing exercises, and progressive muscle relaxation into your daily routine. These techniques help to calm the mind, reduce stress, and improve emotional regulation.

3. **Healthy Lifestyle:** Maintain a healthy lifestyle by prioritizing regular exercise, a balanced diet, and adequate sleep. Physical well-being significantly impacts emotional health, and caring for your body can enhance your emotional resilience.

4. **Emotional Expression:** Allow yourself to express your emotions healthily. Whether through journaling, talking with a trusted friend or mentor, or engaging in creative activities,

expressing emotions can prevent them from building up and causing imbalance.

5. **Setting Boundaries:** Set clear boundaries between work and personal life to prevent burnout and emotional exhaustion. Learn to avoid additional commitments that may overwhelm you and ensure you have time for rest and rejuvenation.

## 4.2 EMOTION MANAGEMENT

Effective emotion management is essential for leaders to navigate the ups and downs of leadership. Here are techniques for managing emotions:

1. **Cognitive Reappraisal:** Practice cognitive reappraisal, which involves changing how you interpret and respond to stressful situations. Instead of viewing a challenge as a threat, reframe it as an opportunity for growth and learning.

2. **Emotion Regulation Strategies:** Use emotion regulation strategies such as positive self-talk, relaxation techniques, and physical activity to manage stress and maintain emotional control. These strategies help to keep your emotions in check and prevent them from negatively impacting your decisions and actions.

3. **Empathy and Active Listening: Show** empathy and practice active listening with your team. Understand and validate their emotions and provide support and reassurance. Empathetic leaders build trust and create a positive work environment where team members feel valued and understood.

4. **Stress-Relief Activities:** Engage in activities that help to relieve stress and improve your mood. Whether exercising, spending time in nature, practicing a hobby, or enjoying time with loved ones, finding ways to relax and recharge is crucial for managing emotions.

5. **Professional Support:** Don't hesitate to seek professional support. Working with a coach, therapist, or counselor can provide valuable insights and strategies for managing emotions and enhancing emotional resilience.

## 4.3 EMPATHY ROLE

Empathy plays a crucial role in emotional resilience and effective leadership. Empathetic leaders can connect with their team members on a deeper level, fostering trust, collaboration, and loyalty. Here's how to integrate empathy into your leadership:

1. **Understanding Empathy:** Empathy is the ability to understand and share the feelings of others. It involves putting yourself in someone else's shoes and seeing the world from their perspective. This understanding helps to build stronger relationships and create a supportive work environment.

2. **Active Listening:** Practice listening by giving your full attention to the speaker, acknowledging their feelings, and responding thoughtfully. Active listening shows that you care about your team members' concerns and are genuinely interested in their well-being.

3. **Emotional Intelligence**: Develop emotional intelligence (EI) by enhancing self-awareness, self-regulation, motivation, empathy, and social skills. High EI enables leaders to navigate social complexities, build strong relationships, and make informed decisions.

4. **Compassionate Leadership:** Lead with compassion by showing kindness and understanding towards your team. Recognize their efforts, celebrate their successes, and provide support during difficult times. Compassionate leadership fosters a positive and resilient organizational culture.

5. **Inclusive Environment**: Create an inclusive environment where diverse perspectives are valued and everyone feels heard and respected. Encourage open communication and provide a safe space for team members to express their thoughts and emotions.

Emotional resilience allows you to connect deeply with your team and maintain stability during turbulent times. You can build a supportive and resilient work environment by cultivating emotional balance, mastering emotion management techniques, and leading with empathy. These skills will enhance your leadership capabilities and foster a culture of trust, collaboration, and mutual respect within your team. Cultivate emotional resilience to lead with strength and compassion, guiding your team through challenges with confidence and grace.

# 5   TEAM RESILIENCE

"The strength of the team is each member. The strength of each member is the team." – Phil Jackson.

A resilient team is a leader's greatest asset. A cohesive and resilient team can adapt, persevere, and thrive in adversity. This chapter focuses on creating a supportive team environment, leveraging diversity, and fostering team resilience. By building a strong, interconnected team, leaders can ensure that their organizations remain robust and capable of overcoming challenges.

Organizations are constantly exposed to various internal and external pressures in today's rapidly changing world. From economic downturns and market shifts to organizational changes and unexpected crises, the ability to withstand and quickly recover from such adversities is paramount. This resilience is the responsibility of the individual leader and the entire team. A resilient team can act as a buffer against the shocks and stresses destabilizing an organization, providing a unified front that can adapt and respond effectively.

Creating a supportive team environment is the foundation of building resilience. It involves fostering a culture where team members feel valued, trusted, and empowered to contribute their best. A supportive environment encourages open communication, mutual respect, and collaboration, all essential for resilience. When team members know they have the backing of their peers and leaders, they are more likely to take initiative, share innovative ideas, and support each other through challenges.

Leveraging diversity within the team is another critical component. Diversity brings a wealth of perspectives, experiences, and skills that can enhance problem-solving and innovation. Teams that embrace diversity are better equipped to tackle complex challenges and develop creative solutions. By valuing and integrating diverse viewpoints, leaders can foster a culture of inclusivity and adaptability, where every team member feels their unique contributions are recognized and appreciated.

Fostering team resilience also requires intentional strategies to support team members through challenges. This involves providing resources, training, and support systems to help team members develop resilience. Leaders play a crucial role in this process by modeling resilient behaviors, offering guidance and encouragement, and creating opportunities for team members to build their resilience skills. This strategic support helps to ensure that team members can cope with current challenges and are prepared to handle future adversities.

In essence, a resilient team is built on the strengths of its members, each of whom contributes their unique skills, perspectives, and resilience to the collective whole. When each member is supported and empowered, the team becomes more robust, more cohesive, and better able to navigate the complexities of the modern organizational landscape. As we delve deeper into this chapter, we will explore practical strategies and real-life examples to help you create a resilient team that can thrive under pressure and drive organizational success.

## 5.1 TEAM ENVIRONMENT

Creating a supportive team environment is the foundation of team resilience. A positive and inclusive environment encourages collaboration, trust, and mutual respect among team members. Here's how to cultivate such an environment:

1. **Psychological Safety:** Foster an atmosphere where team members feel safe to express their thoughts, ask questions, and take risks without fear of ridicule or retribution. Psychological safety is crucial for open communication and innovation. Encourage open and honest communication by creating channels for feedback and discussion. Regular team meetings, one-on-one check-ins, and anonymous feedback tools can

help facilitate open dialogue. Build trust within the team by being transparent, reliable, and consistent. Trust is the bedrock of a resilient team, enabling members to depend on each other and work together effectively. Recognize and appreciate the contributions of team members. Celebrate big and small achievements to boost morale and reinforce a positive team culture.

2. **Collaboration:** Encourage collaboration by encouraging team members to collaborate on projects and problem-solving. Collaborative efforts can enhance creativity, distribute workloads, and strengthen team bonds. Organize team-building activities that promote collaboration and camaraderie. Activities like workshops, retreats, and group challenges can help team members develop a sense of unity and shared purpose. Engage team members in cross-functional projects that require collaboration with different departments or skill sets. This exposure to diverse perspectives can enhance problem-solving and innovation.

3. **Support Systems:** Establish support systems that provide team members with the resources and assistance they need to thrive. Implement mentorship programs that pair experienced team

members with newer or less experienced colleagues. Mentorship can provide guidance, support, and a sense of belonging. Ensure team members can access the tools, training, and resources to perform their roles effectively. Adequate support fosters confidence and resilience.

4. **Supporting Teams:** Supporting teams through challenges requires intentional effort and strategic support. Here's how to effectively support your team:

- **Active Support:** Be proactive in supporting team members during challenging times. This includes offering help, resources, and encouragement to navigate obstacles. Allocate resources strategically to ensure team members have what they need to succeed. This might include additional training, technology, or personnel support. Provide emotional support by showing empathy and understanding. Recognize the emotional impact of challenges and offer a listening ear or counseling resources when needed.

- **Resilience Training:** Equip your team with the skills and knowledge to build resilience. Offer resilience training programs that teach stress management, emotional regulation, and adaptive thinking. These programs can empower team members to handle stress and adversity more effectively. Host workshops and seminars on resilience-related topics, such as mindfulness, positive psychology, and effective communication. Continuous learning opportunities can enhance team resilience.

- **Flexibility and Adaptability:** Encourage flexibility and adaptability within the team. Provide flexible work arrangements, such as remote work options or flexible hours, to accommodate the diverse needs of team members. Flexibility can reduce stress and enhance work-life balance. Encourage the team to adopt adaptive strategies, such as agile project management and iterative problem-solving. An adaptable team can quickly respond to changing circumstances and remain resilient.

- **Feedback and Improvement:** Foster a culture of continuous feedback and improvement. Provide regular, constructive feedback to help team members grow and improve. Feedback should be specific, actionable, and delivered in a supportive manner. Encourage a mindset of continuous improvement by regularly evaluating team processes and performance. Identify areas for enhancement and implement changes to boost efficiency and resilience.

## 5.2 LEVERAGING DIVERSITY

Leveraging diversity within the team can significantly enhance resilience. Diverse teams bring a wide range of perspectives, experiences, and skills, which can lead to more innovative solutions and better problem-solving. Here's how to harness the power of diversity:

1. **Inclusive Leadership:** Practice inclusive leadership by actively seeking and valuing diverse perspectives. Recruit team members from diverse backgrounds to ensure a wide range of experiences and viewpoints. Diverse recruitment can enhance creativity and innovation within the team. Create an inclusive culture where all team members feel valued and respected. Promote inclusivity through policies, practices, and behaviors recognizing and celebrating diversity.

2. **Collaborative Decision-Making:** Involve diverse team members in decision-making to leverage their unique insights. Encourage team members from different backgrounds to

contribute their ideas and perspectives during decision-making. This can lead to more comprehensive and well-rounded decisions. Facilitate collaborative discussions that involve team members with diverse expertise. Diverse input can enhance problem-solving and innovation.

3. **Cultural Competence:** Develop cultural competence by understanding and appreciating team members' diverse backgrounds. Enhance cultural awareness through training and education. Understanding different cultures, traditions, and communication styles can improve interactions and reduce misunderstandings. Practice respectful communication that acknowledges and values team members' diverse perspectives. Effective communication can bridge cultural differences and foster collaboration.

4. **Equity and Inclusion:** Ensure all team members have equal opportunities to contribute and succeed. Provide equitable opportunities for growth, development, and advancement within the team. This can include mentorship programs, professional development, and access to leadership roles. Implement inclusive practices that recognize and address the unique needs of

diverse team members. This can include flexible work arrangements, accessibility accommodations, and inclusive policies.

By leveraging diversity, you can build a resilient team that thrives on each member's strengths and contributions. Diverse teams are more adaptable, innovative, and better equipped to handle challenges.

Building a resilient team requires intentional effort and strategic support. The insights from this chapter will help you foster a team that thrives under pressure. Creating a supportive team environment, providing strategic support, and leveraging diversity can enhance your team's resilience and ensure their success. A resilient team is a powerful asset that can confidently navigate challenges and emerge more substantial together.

# 6  LEARNING FROM FAILURE

"Only those who dare to fail greatly can achieve greatly."
— Robert F. Kennedy.

Failure is not the opposite of success; it's part of the journey. Embracing failure as a learning opportunity is a critical component of resilient leadership. It allows leaders to grow, innovate, and improve continuously. This chapter teaches how to embrace failure, use reflective techniques, and learn from growth examples. By changing our perception of failure, we can turn setbacks into valuable lessons and catalysts for growth, fostering a culture of resilience and continuous improvement within our organizations.

In leadership, failure is often viewed with apprehension and negativity. However, the most successful leaders understand that failure is not a final destination but a necessary stepping stone to success. When leaders embrace failure, they open the door to a world of learning and development that can lead to more significant achievements and innovations. This mindset shift is essential for cultivating resilience, both personally and within the team.

To embrace failure effectively, leaders must first recognize its value. Every failure carries a wealth of information and insights that can illuminate new paths and strategies. Instead of fearing failure, resilient leaders see it as an opportunity to understand better what works and what doesn't. This perspective enables them to make more informed decisions, avoid repeating mistakes, and continuously refine their approaches.

Embracing failure also requires a supportive organizational culture that encourages experimentation and risk-taking. When team members know that their leaders view failure as a learning opportunity rather than a cause for punishment, they are more likely to innovate and take calculated risks. This environment fosters creativity and adaptability, essential traits for navigating the complexities and uncertainties of today's business landscape.

Reflective techniques play a crucial role in learning from failure. By systematically analyzing setbacks and reflecting on the underlying causes and outcomes, leaders can extract valuable lessons and apply them to future endeavors. Techniques such as journaling, after-action reviews, and peer feedback can help individuals and teams process their experiences and identify areas for improvement.

Moreover, learning from growth examples—stories of individuals and organizations that have turned failures into successes—provides practical insights and inspiration. These examples demonstrate that failure is not an endpoint but a precursor to innovation and achievement. By studying these stories, leaders can glean strategies for overcoming obstacles, maintaining resilience, and ultimately achieving greatness.

By changing our perception of failure, we can transform it from a source of fear and discouragement into a powerful tool for growth and development. This chapter will provide the strategies and techniques needed to embrace failure, reflect on it constructively, and learn from it effectively. Doing so will build a culture of resilience and continuous improvement within your organization, ensuring every setback becomes a stepping stone towards tremendous success.

## 6.1 EMBRACING FAILURE

Embracing failure involves changing our mindset to view setbacks as opportunities for learning and growth rather than definitive judgments of our abilities. Here's how to foster a culture that embraces failure:

1. **Normalize Failure:** Encourage a culture where failure is seen as a natural part of the learning process. Share stories of famous failures and how they led to significant breakthroughs. This helps

to demystify failure and reduce the stigma associated with it. Please share your own experiences with failure and what you learned from them. By being open about your failures, you set an example for your team and create an environment where they feel safe to take risks. Recognize and celebrate efforts, even when they don't result in immediate success. Acknowledge the hard work and innovative thinking that went into a project, regardless of the outcome.

2. **Risk-Taking:** Encourage calculated risk-taking by creating an environment where team members feel safe to experiment and innovate without fear of punitive consequences. Foster a supportive environment where team members know mistakes are growth opportunities, not grounds for punishment. This encourages them to push boundaries and explore new ideas. Implement policies that support learning from failure, such as "fail-fast" initiatives or innovation labs where experimentation is encouraged and failures are seen as valuable learning experiences.

3. **Feedback and Reflection:** Make feedback and reflection a regular part of the workflow. Constructive feedback helps individuals understand what went wrong and how they can

improve. Regular Debriefs: Conduct regular debriefs after projects or initiatives to discuss what worked, what didn't, and why. These sessions should be open, non-judgmental, and focused on learning and improvement. Use 360-degree feedback mechanisms to gather insights from multiple perspectives. This comprehensive feedback helps individuals better understand their performance and areas for growth.

## 6.2 REFLECTIVE TECHNIQUES

Reflective techniques are essential for turning failures into learning opportunities. By systematically analyzing setbacks, leaders can extract valuable insights and apply them to future endeavors. Here are some effective reflective techniques:

1. **Journaling:** Encourage team members to keep a reflective journal where they document their experiences, thoughts, and feelings related to their work. Journaling helps individuals process their emotions and identify patterns in their behavior and decision-making. Provide guided prompts to help structure journaling sessions. Questions like "What went well today?" "What challenges did I face?" and "What can I learn from this experience?" can help focus the reflection.

2. **After-Action Reviews (AARs):** Conduct After-Action Reviews to analyze what happened during a project or event, why it happened, and how it can be improved. Use a structured approach for AARs, focusing on critical areas such as objectives, outcomes, processes, and lessons learned. This systematic analysis helps to identify specific actions that can enhance future performance. Encourage collaborative discussions during AARs, involving all team members in the reflection process. This collective reflection fosters a shared understanding and promotes a culture of continuous improvement.

3. **SWOT Analysis:** Use SWOT (Strengths, Weaknesses, Opportunities, Threats) analysis to evaluate a project or decision's outcomes. This technique helps identify internal and external factors influencing the results and provides a framework for future planning. Analyze the team's approach, identifying areas of competence and areas that need improvement. Assess the external opportunities and threats that impacted the project, considering how these factors can be leveraged or mitigated in the future.

4. **Peer Reviews:** Implement peer review sessions where team members review each other's work

and provide constructive feedback. Peer reviews can offer new perspectives and insights that individuals might not have considered. Create an open and honest feedback culture where team members feel comfortable sharing their thoughts and suggestions. This openness promotes mutual learning and growth. Emphasize the goal of peer reviews as an improvement rather than criticism. Feedback should be specific, actionable, and aimed at helping individuals develop their skills.

## 6.3 GROWTH EXAMPLES

Learning from growth examples involves studying how others have turned failures into successes. These examples can serve as inspiration and provide practical lessons for your team. Here are some notable growth examples:

1. **Thomas Edison:** Edison famously said, "I have not failed. I've just found 10,000 ways that won't work." His persistence and willingness to learn from each failure eventually led to the invention of the electric light bulb. Edison's story illustrates the importance of persistence and resilience. Encourage your team to keep trying and learning from cach attempt, knowing that each failure brings them closer to success. Highlight how

Edison's iterative approach to innovation—testing, failing, and refining—can be applied to your team's projects and initiatives.

2. **J.K. Rowling:** Before achieving worldwide success with the Harry Potter series, Rowling faced numerous rejections from publishers. Her perseverance and belief in her work eventually led to one of history's most successful book series. Rowling's experience shows rejection and failure are not the end but a step toward eventual success. Encourage your team to view setbacks as temporary and keep pursuing their goals with determination. Emphasize the importance of believing in one's vision and staying committed to it, even when faced with obstacles and setbacks.

3. **Airbnb:** The founders of Airbnb faced multiple failures and financial struggles before their business model took off. Their ability to learn from each setback and pivot their strategy was critical to their success. Airbnb's story highlights the importance of adaptability and flexibility. Teach your team to be open to change and ready to pivot their approach based on feedback and new insights. Show how Airbnb's focus on understanding and responding to customer feedback helped them refine their product and

achieve success. Encourage your team to seek and use feedback to improve their work actively.

4. **Walt Disney:** Walt Disney was fired from a newspaper job for "lacking imagination" and faced numerous business failures before creating Disneyland and the Disney empire. Disney's story underscores the value of vision and creativity in overcoming failure. Inspire your team to think big and pursue their creative ideas, knowing failure is part of the journey. Highlight Disney's resilience in the face of repeated setbacks and his ability to turn failures into opportunities for more significant achievements.

By studying these growth examples, you can show your team the value of learning from failure and turning setbacks into successes.

Embracing failure as a learning opportunity transforms setbacks into stepping stones. Adopting a mindset that views failure as an integral part of the journey to success can foster a culture of resilience and continuous improvement within your team. Use the strategies and techniques outlined in this chapter to turn failures into catalysts for growth, encouraging your team to take risks, learn from their experiences, and strive for greatness. With the right approach, every failure can bring you one step closer to achieving your goals.

# 7 ADAPTABILITY

"It is not the strongest of the species that survive, nor the most intelligent, but the one most responsive to change."

– Charles Darwin.

Adaptability is essential for thriving in a rapidly changing world. Quickly and effectively adapting is crucial for successful leadership in an era marked by constant innovation, shifting market dynamics, and unforeseen challenges. This chapter explores the importance of adaptability and the techniques for staying flexible and balancing consistency. By developing adaptability, leaders can navigate uncertainties, capitalize on new opportunities, and maintain organizational resilience.

The pace of change in today's business environment is unprecedented. Technological advancements, global economic shifts, regulatory changes, and unexpected crises like the COVID-19 pandemic have highlighted the need for leaders who can pivot and adapt with agility. These challenges require leaders to move beyond traditional management practices and embrace a mindset that welcomes change as an opportunity rather than a threat.

Adaptability in leadership means more than just reacting to change; it involves proactively anticipating shifts and being prepared to respond in ways that leverage new opportunities while mitigating risks. Leaders who cultivate adaptability can guide their organizations through turbulent times, ensuring they remain competitive and relevant. This ability to pivot and adjust strategies swiftly is a nice-to-have skill and a critical competency determining an organization's long-term success and sustainability.

Moreover, adaptable leaders inspire their teams to adopt a similar mindset. When leaders demonstrate flexibility and a positive attitude toward change, they create a culture where innovation and continuous improvement are valued. This environment empowers team members to take initiative, experiment with new ideas, and confidently embrace the unknown. As a result, the organization becomes more resilient and better equipped to handle whatever comes its way.

Leaders must develop specific skills and strategies to thrive in this ever-evolving landscape. This chapter will delve into the importance of adaptability, offering insights into why it is crucial for leadership and organizational success. We will explore practical techniques for staying flexible, from fostering an open mindset to implementing agile practices. Additionally, we will discuss balancing adaptability with consistency, ensuring that the organization's core values and long-term vision remain intact even as strategies and operations evolve.

By the end of this chapter, you will have a deeper understanding of how to cultivate adaptability within yourself and your team. You will learn how to embrace change proactively, harness the power of flexibility, and maintain a steady course amidst the chaos. These skills will enhance your effectiveness as a leader and position your organization to thrive in a world where change is the only constant.

### 7.1 IMPORTANCE OF ADAPTABILITY

Adaptability is the capacity to adjust to new conditions and respond effectively to changes. It is a critical component of resilience and a key determinant of success in today's dynamic environment. Here's why adaptability is essential for leaders:

1. **Navigating Uncertainty**: Leaders must navigate uncertainty confidently in a world where change is the only constant. Adaptable leaders can quickly assess new situations, determine the best action, and implement changes effectively. The ability to pivot strategies and adapt to new realities is essential during crises. Adaptable leaders can lead teams through turbulent times by

staying calm, flexible, and proactive. Change often brings new opportunities. Adaptable leaders can recognize and seize these opportunities, positioning their organizations for growth and success.

2. **Driving Innovation:** Adaptability fosters a culture of innovation by encouraging leaders and their teams to experiment, take risks, and embrace new ideas. Adaptable leaders are committed to continuous improvement. They encourage their teams to learn from experiences, iterate on processes, and strive for better outcomes. An adaptable mindset supports creativity and innovation. Leaders who embrace change inspire their teams to think outside the box and develop innovative solutions.

3. **Building Resilience:** Adaptability enhances organizational resilience by enabling leaders to respond effectively to changes and disruptions. Adaptable leaders implement agile strategies that allow their organizations to respond quickly to market changes, technological advancements, and other external factors. When leaders model adaptability, they foster a culture of resilience within their teams. Engaged employees who feel

supported in adapting to change are more likely to stay motivated and perform at their best.

## 7.2 STAYING FLEXIBLE

Staying flexible involves cultivating an open mindset and developing strategies to respond effectively to change. Here are techniques for staying flexible:

1. **Open Mindset:** Embrace an open mindset by being receptive to new ideas, perspectives, and ways of doing things. Commit to lifelong learning by seeking out new knowledge and experiences. Attend workshops, read books, and engage with thought leaders in your field to stay informed about the latest trends and developments. Accept that uncertainty is a natural part of life and leadership. Develop a positive attitude towards uncertainty by viewing it as an opportunity for growth and discovery.

2. **Agile Practices:** Implement agile practices that promote flexibility and responsiveness. Use iterative processes like the agile methodology to break down projects into manageable phases. Regularly review and adjust plans based on feedback and changing conditions. Form cross-functional teams that bring together diverse skills and perspectives. These teams can adapt more

quickly to changing requirements and collaborate effectively to achieve goals.

3. **Scenario Planning:** Use scenario planning to prepare for future events. Develop multiple scenarios that consider different potential outcomes. This proactive approach helps you anticipate changes and develop strategies to address them. Ensure that your plans are flexible and can be adjusted as new information becomes available. Avoid rigid planning that doesn't allow for adaptability.

4. **Empowerment and Autonomy:** Empower your team members to make decisions and take ownership of their work. Delegate authority to team members, allowing them to respond quickly to changes without waiting for top-down directives. This autonomy fosters a sense of responsibility and initiative. Create a supportive environment where team members feel confident in adapting. Provide the necessary resources, training, and encouragement to help them succeed.

## 7.3 BALANCING CONSISTENCY

While adaptability is crucial, it is also essential to balance it with consistency. Consistency provides stability and clarity, essential for maintaining trust and achieving long-term goals. Here's how to balance adaptability with consistency:

1. **Core Values and Vision:** Maintain a clear focus on your organization's core values and vision, even as you adapt to changing circumstances. Ensure that your core values serve as guiding principles for decision-making. These values provide a stable foundation that can guide your organization through periods of change. Continuously align your strategies and actions with your organization's vision. This alignment ensures that your adaptations support your long-term goals and mission.

2. **Transparent Communication:** Communicate changes transparently to your team, explaining the reasons behind adaptations and how they align with the organization's goals. Foster an open dialogue with your team, encouraging questions and feedback. Transparent communication builds trust and ensures that everyone understands the rationale for changes. Provide consistent messaging that reinforces your organization's values and vision. This consistency helps to maintain a sense of stability even during periods of change.

3. **Standard Operating Procedures**: Maintain standard operating procedures (SOPs) for routine tasks while allowing flexibility for innovation and improvement. Document key processes to provide a clear framework for how things should be done. This documentation ensures that essential tasks are carried out consistently. Regularly review and update SOPs to incorporate new learnings and improvements. This approach ensures that your processes remain relevant and compelling while allowing adaptability.

4. **Performance Metrics:** Use performance metrics to track progress and ensure that adaptations lead to desired outcomes. Define clear performance metrics that align with your organization's goals. These metrics provide a benchmark for evaluating the effectiveness of your adaptations. Regular evaluations should be conducted to assess progress and identify areas for improvement. Use these evaluations to make data-driven decisions and refine your strategies.

Balancing adaptability with consistency allows you to navigate change effectively while maintaining a stable organizational foundation. This balance ensures you remain agile and responsive without losing sight of your core values and long-term goals.

Cultivating adaptability ensures you remain practical and relevant as a leader. Adapting quickly and effectively is a powerful asset in a world of inevitable change. Embrace change and lead with agility, using the strategies outlined in this chapter to stay flexible and balanced. You can build a resilient organization that thrives in any environment by fostering an adaptable mindset and supporting your team in navigating change.

# 8 PERFORMANCE UNDER PRESSURE

"Pressure makes diamonds." – George S. Patton.

Performing under pressure distinguishes great leaders. In the high-stakes environment of modern leadership, maintaining composure and delivering results under pressure is a critical skill. This chapter provides strategies for maintaining high performance, effective time management, and building endurance. By mastering these techniques, leaders can survive and thrive in demanding situations, turning pressure into an opportunity for excellence and growth.

Pressure is an inevitable part of leadership. From tight deadlines and high expectations to unforeseen crises and complex decision-making, leaders are constantly faced with situations that test their resilience and capabilities. The metaphor of pressure creating diamonds perfectly encapsulates the potential for transformation that pressure can bring. Just as diamonds are formed under intense heat and pressure, great leaders are often forged through their ability to perform under demanding conditions.

Maintaining composure is paramount in high-pressure environments. Composure allows leaders to think, make informed decisions, and inspire team confidence. It's not just about staying calm on the surface but about developing an inner resilience that enables consistent performance regardless of external stressors. Leaders who manage their emotions and focus under pressure are better equipped to guide their organizations through challenging times.

Delivering results under pressure is another hallmark of effective leadership. It's about executing strategies efficiently, managing resources wisely, and achieving goals despite the challenges. High performance under pressure requires technical and strategic skills, a strong mindset, and well-developed coping mechanisms. Leaders must be able to prioritize tasks, delegate effectively, and stay organized to ensure that their teams remain productive and motivated.

This chapter will explore various strategies to help leaders excel under pressure. We will discuss techniques for maintaining high performance, such as prioritization and stress management, which are crucial for staying focused and productive. Effective time management strategies, including planning, delegation, and using productivity tools, will also be covered to help leaders make the most of their available time and resources.

Building endurance is another critical aspect of performing under pressure. Endurance involves developing the physical and mental stamina needed to sustain high performance over extended periods. We will delve into practices that enhance physical fitness, mental resilience, and sustainable work habits, all of which contribute to a leader's ability to perform consistently under pressure.

By mastering these techniques, leaders can transform pressure from a source of stress into an opportunity for growth and excellence. High-pressure situations, while challenging, can also be advantageous, offering leaders the chance to demonstrate their capabilities and achieve significant accomplishments. Through the strategies outlined in this chapter, you will learn how to harness the power of pressure to elevate your leadership performance and drive your organization toward success.

## 8.1 MAINTAINING PERFORMANCE

Maintaining performance under pressure involves staying focused, calm, and effective despite the challenges. Here are strategies to help you maintain high performance:

1. **Prioritization:** Focus on the most critical tasks first. When under pressure, it's essential to identify the tasks that will have the most significant impact and prioritize them. Use the

Eisenhower Matrix to categorize tasks into four quadrants: urgent and important, important but not urgent, urgent but not necessary, and neither urgent nor essential. This helps to prioritize tasks effectively. Set clear objectives for what needs to be accomplished. A clear understanding of your goals can help you stay focused and avoid distractions.

2. **Stress Management:** Implement techniques to maintain calm and clarity. Practice mindfulness and meditation to reduce stress and increase focus. Even a few minutes of deep breathing or meditation can significantly lower stress levels. Take regular breaks to prevent burnout. Frequent breaks can help refresh your mind and maintain high productivity levels.

3. **Focus and Concentration:** Develop strategies to enhance focus and concentration. Use the Pomodoro Technique to break work into intervals, typically 25 minutes of focused work followed by a 5-minute break. This method can improve concentration and productivity. Identify and minimize distractions in your environment. This may involve creating a quiet workspace, turning off notifications, or setting specific times for checking emails.

4. **Emotional Regulation:** Maintain emotional balance to ensure clear thinking and decision-making. Practice cognitive reappraisal to reinterpret stressful situations in a more positive light. Viewing challenges as opportunities for growth can help maintain a positive mindset. Lean on your support systems-mentors, colleagues, or family. Having a network of support can provide emotional stability and practical advice.

## 8.2 TIME MANAGEMENT

Effective time management is crucial for maintaining performance under pressure. Here are techniques to help you manage your time efficiently:

1. **Planning and Scheduling:** Plan and schedule your tasks to ensure you use your time effectively. Start each day with a clear plan of what needs to be accomplished. List your tasks and prioritize them based on importance and deadlines. Use time blocking to allocate specific periods for different tasks. This helps ensure you dedicate adequate time to each task and avoid multitasking.

2. **Delegation:** Delegate tasks to team members to ensure that you focus on high-priority activities.

Identify tasks that can be delegated to others. This frees up your time to focus on tasks that require your unique expertise. Empower your team members by providing clear instructions and the necessary resources. Trust them to handle the tasks effectively.

3. **Efficiency Tools:** Use tools and techniques to enhance your efficiency. For example, use task management apps like Trello, Asana, or Monday.com to organize tasks and track progress. These tools can help you stay organized and on top of your workload. Automate repetitive tasks where possible. Automation tools can save time and reduce the cognitive load.

4. **Time Audits**: Conduct regular time audits to identify where your time is going and make adjustments as needed. Track how you spend your time over a week. Identify activities that are taking up more time than they should. Use the insights from your time audit to adjust your priorities and allocate more time to high-value activities.

## 8.3 BUILDING ENDURANCE

Building endurance involves developing the physical and mental stamina needed to sustain high performance over extended periods. Here are strategies to build endurance:

1. **Physical Fitness:** Maintain physical fitness to enhance energy levels and overall resilience. Incorporate regular exercise into your routine. Running, cycling, and strength training can improve physical endurance and reduce stress. Eat a balanced diet that gives your body the nutrients it needs to function optimally. Avoid excessive caffeine and sugar, which can lead to energy crashes.

2. **Mental Resilience:** Develop mental resilience to cope with prolonged stress and pressure. Cultivate a growth mindset that views challenges as opportunities for development. This mindset can enhance your resilience and ability to persevere through difficulties. Practice stress-relief techniques such as yoga, meditation, and deep breathing. These practices can help you manage stress and maintain mental clarity.

3. **Sleep and Recovery:** Prioritize sleep and recovery to ensure your body and mind are well-rested. Aim for 7-9 hours of sleep each night. Quality sleep is essential for cognitive function,

emotional regulation, and physical health— schedule rest days to allow your body and mind to recover from intense work periods. Recovery is crucial for maintaining long-term performance.

4. **Sustainable Work Practices:** Develop work practices that support long-term sustainability. Pace yourself during high-pressure periods. Avoid the temptation to work at maximum intensity continuously, as this can lead to burnout. Ensure that your workload is balanced and manageable. Avoid overcommitting and recognize when to scale back or seek additional support.

Performance under pressure requires preparation and resilience. Applying this chapter's strategies allows you to excel even in the most demanding situations. Maintaining high performance, managing your time effectively, and building endurance will equip you with the tools to thrive under pressure. Embrace the challenges of high-pressure environments and use them as opportunities to demonstrate your strength, resilience, and leadership capabilities.

# 9  TOUGH COMMUNICATION

"The single biggest problem in communication is the illusion that it has taken place." – George Bernard Shaw.

Challenging communication is an inevitable part of leadership. Leaders frequently face situations that require difficult conversations, whether it's delivering critical feedback, managing conflicts, or communicating bad news. Handling these conversations effectively is crucial for maintaining trust, fostering a positive work environment, and ensuring that the organization operates smoothly. This chapter offers practical strategies for difficult conversations, maintaining trust, and delivering inspirational talks. By mastering these communication techniques, leaders can navigate challenging situations confidently and clearly, turning potential conflicts into opportunities for growth and understanding.

Communication is the bedrock of effective leadership. However, as George Bernard Shaw aptly pointed out, one of the biggest problems in communication is the illusion that it has occurred. Leaders often assume that their messages are clear and understood, but this assumption can lead to misunderstandings, frustration, and even conflict. Challenging communication, in particular, requires a heightened level of clarity, empathy, and strategic thinking.

Difficult conversations are inevitable in any leadership role. These can range from providing constructive feedback to addressing performance issues, handling interpersonal conflicts, or delivering unwelcome news about organizational changes or layoffs. These conversations are challenging because they touch on sensitive topics and can evoke strong emotions. Yet, they are essential for the growth and functioning of individuals and the organization. When handled poorly, tough conversations can damage relationships and trust. However, they can strengthen bonds, clarify expectations, and drive improvement when approached with skill and empathy.

Maintaining trust during tough conversations is paramount. Trust is the foundation of any effective relationship and is particularly critical in the workplace. Employees must feel that their leaders are honest and fair and have their best interests at heart. Trust is built through consistent, transparent communication and is maintained by demonstrating respect and empathy, even in the most challenging discussions. Leaders who can navigate these conversations effectively can preserve and even enhance trust, fostering a more resilient and cohesive team.

Delivering inspirational talks is another aspect of challenging communication. Whether it's rallying the team during a challenging project, motivating them to embrace change, or inspiring them to strive for higher performance, leaders must communicate in uplifting and energizing ways. Inspirational communication involves more than words; it requires authenticity, emotional connection, and a clear vision. Practical, inspirational talks can transform challenging situations into collective growth and innovation opportunities.

This chapter delves into the strategies and techniques necessary for mastering challenging communication. We will explore methods for preparing and conducting difficult conversations with clarity and empathy, techniques for maintaining and building trust during these interactions, and approaches for delivering inspirational and motivating talks. By the end of this chapter, you will be equipped with the tools and insights needed to handle challenging communication with confidence and effectiveness, ensuring that even the most challenging discussions lead to positive outcomes for your team and organization.

## 9.1 EFFECTIVE STRATEGIES

Effective communication strategies are essential for handling challenging conversations. These strategies help ensure the message is delivered respectfully and constructively. Here are some critical approaches:

1.  **Preparation:** Before engaging in a difficult conversation, take the time to prepare. Understand the issue, gather relevant information, and plan your approach. Clearly define the purpose of the conversation. Know what you want to achieve and the key points you must address. Consider how the other person might react and prepare for different scenarios. This helps you remain calm and composed during the conversation.

2.  **Active Listening:** Practice listening to understand the other person's perspective. This involves giving your full attention, acknowledging their feelings, and responding thoughtfully. Demonstrate empathy by acknowledging the other person's emotions and concerns. Statements like "I understand how you feel" can help build rapport and trust. Reflect on what you hear to ensure understanding and clarify any ambiguities. This shows that you value their input and are genuinely interested in their perspective.

3.  **Clear and Direct Communication:** Be clear and direct. Avoid vague language and get to the point while remaining respectful and considerate.

Use "I" statements to express your feelings and perspectives without sounding accusatory. For example, "I feel concerned when..." instead of "You always..." Keep the conversation focused on the issue at hand. Avoid bringing up unrelated topics or past grievances that can derail the discussion.

4. **Stay Calm and Composed:** Maintain your composure, even if the conversation becomes heated. Keeping calm helps to de-escalate tension and fosters a more productive dialogue. If you feel emotions rising, take a moment to pause and breathe. This helps to calm your mind and allows you to respond more thoughtfully. Even in disagreement, remain respectful. Avoid personal attacks or inflammatory language that can damage the relationship.

5. **Seek Solutions:** Aim to find a mutually beneficial solution. Collaborate with the other person to identify actions that address the issue and support both parties' needs. Engage in problem-solving rather than blaming. Focus on what can be done to improve the situation moving forward. Conclude the conversation with clear, agreed-upon actions. Ensure that both parties

understand what needs to be done and are committed to following through.

## 9.2 MAINTAINING TRUST

Maintaining trust is crucial during tough conversations. Trust is the foundation of effective communication and a healthy organizational culture. Here's how to maintain and build trust:

1. **Transparency:** Be transparent in your communication. Share information openly and honestly, even when the news is difficult. Always be truthful, even if it means delivering bad news. People are more likely to trust you if they know you are honest and straightforward. Be consistent in your actions and words. Consistency builds credibility and trust over time.

2. **Follow-Through:** Ensure you follow through on commitments during tough conversations. Hold yourself accountable for the commitments you make. Follow through on your promises and demonstrate reliability. Schedule follow-up meetings to check on progress and address any ongoing concerns. Regular check-ins show that you are committed to resolving the issue.

3. **Respect:** Respect the other person's feelings, perspectives, and dignity. Approach conversations

with empathy and a willingness to understand the other person's point of view. This respect fosters trust and collaboration. Treat everyone fairly and without favoritism. Fairness in your actions and decisions builds trust across the organization.

4. **Confidentiality:** Maintain confidentiality where appropriate. Respecting privacy builds trust and encourages open communication. Handle sensitive information with care and discretion. Ensure that confidential matters are discussed privately and not shared inappropriately. Communicate boundaries regarding confidentiality to set expectations for both parties.

## 9.3 INSPIRATIONAL TALKS

Inspirational talks can uplift and motivate your team, especially during challenging times. Here are strategies for delivering impactful and inspiring messages:

1. **Purposeful Messaging:** Ensure your message has a clear purpose and resonates with your audience. Understand your audience's needs, concerns, and aspirations. Tailor your message to address these elements effectively. Identify the key takeaways you want your audience to remember. Focus on these points to create a lasting impact.

2. **Storytelling:** Use storytelling to connect with your audience emotionally. Stories can illustrate key points and make your message more relatable and memorable. Share personal stories and experiences that highlight your message. Authentic stories can inspire and build a deeper connection with your audience. Highlight success stories within your organization or industry to demonstrate what is possible and inspire your team to strive for excellence.

3. **Positive Language:** Use positive and empowering language to motivate your audience. Encourage your team by recognizing their efforts and potential. Statements like "I believe in you" and "We can achieve this together" can boost morale. Clearly articulate your vision and the goals you aim to achieve. Inspire your team by painting a compelling picture of the future and their role in it.

4. **Engagement:** Engage your audience by encouraging interaction and participation. Invite questions and feedback during your talk. This interaction shows that you value your audience's input and fosters collaboration. End your talk with a clear call to action. Inspire your team to take specific steps toward achieving your goals.

5.  **Authenticity:** Be authentic and genuine in your delivery. Authenticity builds trust and makes your message more powerful. Let your true self shine through in your communication. Authenticity resonates with people and makes your message more credible. Speak with passion and conviction. Your enthusiasm can be contagious and inspire your team to share your vision.

Mastering challenging communication builds trust and clarity. Applying the techniques outlined in this chapter, you can confidently navigate challenging conversations and maintain strong, trusting relationships with your team. Effective communication is a hallmark of outstanding leadership, particularly during difficult times. Use these strategies to turn challenging conversations into opportunities for growth and collaboration and deliver inspirational talks that motivate and uplift your team.

# 10 FUTURE PATH

"Do not go where the path may lead; go instead where there is no path and leave a trail." – Ralph Waldo Emerson.

The journey of resilience doesn't end; it evolves. As leaders, pursuing resilience is a continuous process that requires ongoing effort and commitment. This chapter discusses integrating resilience into everyday leadership, fostering continuous development, and inspiring others. By embracing resilience as a core aspect of your leadership style, you can confidently navigate future challenges, drive innovation, and inspire those around you to reach their full potential. The principles and strategies you have learned throughout this book are not just tools for today but foundational practices that will support your growth and effectiveness as a leader in the long term.

Leadership in the modern world is akin to forging new paths in uncharted territories. The landscape of business and organizations is constantly changing, and the ability to adapt, innovate, and inspire is more critical than ever. Resilience is the compass that guides leaders through these uncharted territories, enabling them to not only survive but thrive amidst challenges and uncertainties.

Resilience is not a static trait but a dynamic continual growth and adaptation process. Each challenge you face and overcome adds to your reservoir of resilience, equipping you with the strength and wisdom to handle future obstacles. As you continue on your leadership journey, it is essential to integrate resilience into your everyday practices. This integration ensures that resilience becomes second nature, a fundamental part of your leadership identity.

Continuous development is critical to maintaining and enhancing resilience. The world does not stand still, and neither should you. Embracing a lifelong learning and self-improvement mindset will keep you ahead of the curve, ready to tackle new challenges confidently. Investing in your personal and professional growth enhances your resilience and sets a powerful example for your team.

Inspiring others is perhaps the most significant aspect of resilient leadership. Demonstrating resilience in your actions and fostering a resilient culture can empower your team to develop their resilience. This collective resilience creates a supportive and adaptive organizational environment where everyone can thrive.

The strategies and principles outlined in this book are designed to help you build and sustain resilience. They are not just quick fixes for immediate problems but foundational practices supporting your long-term growth as a leader. By consistently applying these strategies, you will cultivate a resilient mindset that enables you to navigate the complexities of leadership with grace and effectiveness.

As we delve into the final chapter, we will explore how to integrate resilience into your everyday leadership practices, foster continuous development, and inspire those around you. These insights will help you chart your unique path forward, leaving a trail of resilience, innovation, and inspiration for others.

## 10.1 INTEGRATING RESILIENCE

Integrating resilience into everyday leadership is fundamental to leading and managing your team. Here's how to embed resilience into your leadership practices:

1. **Lead by Example:** Demonstrate resilience in your behavior. Show your team how to respond to challenges with a positive attitude and proactive approach. Consistently model resilient behaviors such as adaptability, persistence, and emotional regulation. Your actions set the tone for your team's response to adversity. Be transparent about your challenges and how you overcome

them. Sharing your experiences can inspire and guide your team.

2. **Resilient Culture:** Foster a culture of resilience within your organization. Create an environment where taking calculated risks and learning from mistakes is safe. Encourage innovation and experimentation without fear of failure. Build a supportive environment where team members feel valued and heard. Provide resources and support to help them develop their resilience.

3. **Resilience Training:** Implement resilience training programs to equip your team with the skills to handle stress and adversity. Offer workshops and seminars on stress management, emotional intelligence, and adaptive thinking. Encourage ongoing learning and development in resilience. Provide access to resources such as books, courses, and mentorship programs.

4. **Feedback and Reflection:** Regularly seek feedback and reflect on your leadership practices to improve your resilience approach. Use 360-degree feedback to gather insights from your team and peers. This comprehensive feedback can highlight areas for growth and development. Engage in regular self-reflection to assess your progress and identify areas for improvement.

Journaling and meditation can be helpful tools for this practice.

## 10.2 CONTINUOUS DEVELOPMENT

Continuous development is essential for maintaining and enhancing your resilience as a leader. Here are strategies to ensure ongoing growth and development:

1. **Lifelong Learning:** Commit to lifelong learning by staying informed about new developments in your field and continually seeking to expand your knowledge and skills. Participate in professional development opportunities such as conferences, workshops, and certification programs. Stay updated with the latest research and literature in leadership and resilience. Read books, articles, and journals to keep your knowledge current.

2. **Skill Enhancement:** Continuously enhance your leadership skills, particularly resilience-related ones. Focus on developing your emotional intelligence, including self-awareness, self-regulation, empathy, and social skills. Cultivate adaptability by exposing yourself to new experiences and challenges. Step out of your comfort zone to develop flexibility and resilience.

3. **Networking:** Build and maintain a solid professional network. Networking provides

101

opportunities for learning, collaboration, and support. Seek out mentors who can provide guidance and perspective. Also, consider mentoring others to share your knowledge and experience. Join peer groups or professional associations where you can share experiences and learn from others in your field.

4. **Self-Care:** Prioritize self-care to maintain your physical and mental well-being. A healthy leader is more resilient and better equipped to handle challenges. Maintain a healthy lifestyle with regular exercise, a balanced diet, and adequate sleep: practice mindfulness, meditation, and other stress-relief techniques to support your mental health and resilience.

## 10.3 INSPIRING OTHERS

Inspiring others to develop their resilience is a crucial aspect of resilient leadership. Here's how to motivate and guide your team:

1. **Vision and Purpose:** Communicate a clear vision and purpose that inspires and motivates your team. Align your team around shared goals and a common purpose. This sense of direction fosters unity and resilience. Craft and communicate an inspiring future vision that

excites and motivates your team to strive for excellence.

2. **Empowerment**: Empower your team members to take ownership of their work and develop resilience. Provide autonomy and encourage initiative. Allow team members to take responsibility for their projects and decisions. Support their development by providing opportunities for learning and growth. Offer training, coaching, and mentorship to help them build their resilience.

3. **Recognition and Encouragement:** Recognize and celebrate your team's achievements and efforts. Encouragement boosts morale and reinforces resilient behaviors. Acknowledge individual and team accomplishments. Celebrate successes and milestones to foster a positive and resilient culture. Provide positive feedback and encouragement regularly. Highlight strengths and potential to inspire confidence and resilience.

4. **Modeling Resilience:** Be a role model of resilience for your team. Your behavior and attitude set the standard for how your team responds to challenges. Maintain a positive attitude and demonstrate resilience in your actions. Your example will inspire your team to

adopt a similar approach. Be open about your challenges and how you overcome them. Sharing your resilience journey can motivate others to develop their own.

Resilience is a lifelong pursuit. It is not a destination but a continuous growth, learning, and adaptation journey. As you progress in your leadership journey, continue developing your resilience, inspiring others, and leading with unwavering strength and vision. The strategies and principles outlined in this book are designed to support you in this ongoing endeavor. Embrace the challenges and opportunities that come your way, and use them as stepping stones to tremendous success and fulfillment. You will create a legacy of strength, adaptability, and enduring leadership by fostering resilience in yourself and those around you.

# CONCLUSION

"Success is to be measured not so much by the position that one has reached in life as by the obstacles which he has overcome." – Booker T. Washington.

As we conclude this exploration of resilient leadership, let's recap the key concepts and look forward to the ongoing journey of growth and development. The path to becoming a resilient leader is marked by continuous learning, self-reflection, and adaptation. The strategies and principles outlined in this book are designed to help you navigate the complexities of leadership with strength and grace. By embracing these practices, you are well-equipped to overcome obstacles, drive innovation, and inspire those around you.

## RECAP OF CONCEPTS

Throughout this book, we have delved into various aspects of resilient leadership, each chapter building on the last to provide a comprehensive guide to developing and sustaining resilience. Here are the key concepts we have explored:

1. **Defining Resilience:** We began by understanding the core of resilience in leadership—its impact, significance, and the stories of leaders who exemplified resilience. We

defined resilience as the capacity to recover quickly from difficulties and adapt to change.

2. **Personal Resilience:** Building personal resilience is the foundation of resilient leadership. We discussed strategies for managing stress, cultivating a resilient mindset, and maintaining emotional balance through self-awareness, mindfulness, and healthy lifestyle choices.

3. **Crisis Leadership:** Effective crisis leadership requires navigating uncertainty, making decisive decisions under pressure, and communicating clearly during crises. We explored case studies and techniques for managing crises with calm and clarity.

4. **Emotional Resilience:** Emotional resilience is critical for maintaining empathy and balance as a leader. We covered techniques for emotional management, the role of empathy, and how to foster emotional resilience within your team.

5. **Team Resilience:** A resilient team is a leader's greatest asset. We focused on creating a supportive team environment, leveraging diversity, and fostering team resilience through trust, collaboration, and continuous support.

6. **Learning from Failure:** Embracing failure as a learning opportunity is essential for growth. We

discussed reflective techniques and shared growth examples to illustrate how setbacks can be transformed into stepping stones for success.

7. **Adaptability:** Adaptability is crucial for thriving in a rapidly changing world. We examined the importance of staying flexible, balancing consistency, and integrating adaptability into leadership practices.

8. **Performance Under Pressure:** Performing under pressure distinguishes great leaders. We provided strategies for maintaining high performance, effective time management, and building endurance to excel in demanding situations.

9. **Tough Communication:** Tough communication is an inevitable part of leadership. We offered practical strategies for difficult conversations, maintaining trust, and delivering inspirational talks to navigate challenging situations confidently.

10. **Future Path:** The journey of resilience is ongoing. We discussed integrating resilience into everyday leadership, fostering continuous development, and inspiring others. These practices ensure that resilience becomes a core aspect of your leadership style.

## ONGOING BUILDING

The journey towards resilient leadership is a continuous process. Here are steps to ensure ongoing growth and development:

1. **Continuous Learning:** Commit to lifelong learning. Stay informed about the latest developments in leadership and resilience. Engage in professional development opportunities, read extensively, and seek new experiences that challenge and expand your capabilities.

2. **Self-Reflection:** Regularly reflect on your experiences and leadership practices. Self-reflection helps you identify areas for improvement and reinforce successful strategies. Consider keeping a journal to document your reflections and track your progress.

3. **Mentorship and Networking:** Seek mentorship and build a solid professional network. Mentors can provide valuable guidance and insights, while a robust network offers support and opportunities for collaboration and growth.

4. **Feedback and Adaptation:** Continuously seek feedback from your team, peers, and mentors. Use this feedback to adapt and refine your

leadership approach. Embrace change and be willing to pivot strategies as needed to stay effective.

5. **Inspire and Empower:** Focus on inspiring and empowering your team. Emphasize their crucial role in developing their resilience and supporting their growth. A resilient team that feels valued and integral is better equipped to handle challenges and drive the organization forward.

6. **Maintain Balance:** Ensure that you maintain a healthy work-life balance. Highlight the personal benefits of self-care and well-being, such as sustained energy and resilience. A balanced leader, feeling motivated and well-cared for, is more effective and better able to support their team.

Your journey towards resilient leadership is transformative. The principles and strategies in this guide will help you navigate leadership with resilience and grace. Keep building, growing, and staying resilient. View challenges as opportunities for growth and innovation. Embrace them confidently, inspire others, and lead with unwavering strength and vision. I look forward to the next installment in the 'Leadership Transformed' series, exploring new dimensions of effective leadership.

# APPENDICES

The appendices are additional resources and a comprehensive support system to bolster your journey toward resilient leadership. Here, you will find practical exercises meticulously designed to help you develop and strengthen resilience, a curated list of further reading materials to deepen your understanding, and references to all the sources cited throughout this book. These resources are tools and a testament to your preparedness and confidence in your growth and development as a resilient leader.

## EXERCISES

Practical exercises are not just the backbone but the essence of developing leadership resilience. They are not just theoretical concepts but tangible tools that can be readily applied in real-world scenarios. Here are some exercises to help you construct and maintain resilience, ensuring that you are not just prepared but equipped to face any challenge:

1. **Mindfulness Meditation:** To enhance self-awareness and emotional regulation. Set aside 10-15 minutes each day for mindfulness meditation. Sit comfortably, close your eyes, and focus on your breath. When your mind wanders, gently

bring your focus back to your breath. This practice helps reduce stress and improve emotional balance.

2. **Journaling:** To reflect on experiences and identify patterns in behavior and responses. Dedicate time each evening to journal about your day. Reflect on your challenges, how you responded, and what you learned. Consider using prompts like "What went well today?" and "What could I have done differently?"

3. **After-Action Reviews (AARs):** These are not just post-project discussions but systematic analyses and learning opportunities. After completing a significant project or event, conduct an AAR. Gather your team and discuss what happened, what went well, what didn't, and how you can improve. Document the insights and apply them to future projects. This is not just a process but a powerful tool for continuous improvement.

4. **SWOT Analysis:** To evaluate personal and team strengths, weaknesses, opportunities, and threats. Perform a SWOT analysis periodically to assess your leadership and team dynamics. Identify areas for improvement and develop action plans to address them.

5. **Scenario Planning:** To prepare for potential challenges and develop adaptive strategies, identify scenarios that could impact your organization. Outline possible responses and strategies for each scenario. Review and update these plans regularly as new information becomes available.

6. **Feedback Sessions:** To gather constructive feedback for continuous improvement. Schedule regular feedback sessions with your team and peers. Encourage honest and constructive feedback, and use it to refine your leadership approach. Reflect on the feedback and create action plans to address identified areas.

## RESOURCES

Further reading and additional resources can deepen your understanding of resilience and leadership. Here are some recommended books, articles, and online resources:

**Books:**

- "Resilience: Hard-Won Wisdom for Living a Better Life" by Eric Greitens
- "The Resilient Leader: How Adversity Can Unlock Your Greatest Potential" by Al Siebert

- "Grit: The Power of Passion and Perseverance" by Angela Duckworth
- "Emotional Intelligence 2.0" by Travis Bradberry and Jean Greaves

**Articles:**

- "How Resilience Works" by Diane Coutu, Harvard Business Review
- "The Role of Emotional Resilience in Leadership" by Amy Morin, Forbes
- "Building the Emotional Intelligence of Groups" by Vanessa Urch Druskat and Steven B. Wolff, Harvard Business Review

**Online Resources:**

- Mindful.org: Offers resources on mindfulness practices to enhance emotional resilience.
- American Psychological Association (APA): Provides articles and tools on resilience and stress management.
- Coursera and edX: Platforms offer leadership, resilience, and emotional intelligence courses.

**REFERENCES**

The following is a list of references and sources cited in this book. These references provide the foundation for the concepts and strategies discussed and offer additional insights for further exploration:

**Books and Articles:**

- Duckworth, Angela. Grit: The Power of Passion and Perseverance. Scribner, 2016.
- Greitens, Eric. Resilience: Hard-Won Wisdom for Living a Better Life. Houghton Mifflin Harcourt, 2015.
- Coutu, Diane. "How Resilience Works." Harvard Business Review, May 2002.
- Morin, Amy. "The Role of Emotional Resilience in Leadership." Forbes, April 2018.

**Research Studies:**

- Siebert, Al. The Resilient Leader: How Adversity Can Unlock Your Greatest Potential. 2005.
- Bradberry, Travis, and Greaves, Jean. Emotional Intelligence 2.0. Talent Smart, 2009.

**Online Articles and Courses:**

- Mindful.org. "Mindfulness Practices for Leaders." Accessed January 2024.
- American Psychological Association. "Building Resilience." Accessed January 2024.

- Coursera. "Leadership and Emotional Intelligence." Accessed January 2024.

Your journey towards resilient leadership is just beginning. The exercises, resources, and references provided in this appendix are tools to support your continuous growth and development. Keep building your resilience, growing as a leader, and staying committed to resilient leadership principles. Embrace challenges as opportunities for learning and growth, and inspire those around you with your unwavering strength and vision. I look forward to the next installment in the "Leadership Transformed" series, where we will explore new dimensions of effective and transformative leadership.

"The greatest use of life is to spend it for something that will outlast it." – William James.

As we near the completion of the "Leadership Transformed" series, the eighth and final book will center on the ultimate goal of many leaders: creating a lasting, positive legacy. This forthcoming book will explore how leaders can shape their actions and strategies to leave a meaningful and enduring impact on their personal and professional spheres.

Key Themes:

- **Defining Your Legacy:** Understand the essence of creating a legacy and align your goals with the impact you wish to leave behind.
- **Visionary Leadership:** Develop and communicate a compelling vision that inspires others and ensures lasting influence.
- **Impactful Actions:** Identify strategies to leverage your strengths and resources to build a lasting impact.
- **Inspiring Change:** Lead transformative change within your organization and community by fostering a culture of innovation and collaboration.

- **Mentorship and Empowerment:** Learn to mentor and empower others to advance your vision and values, creating a ripple effect of positive influence.
- **Sustaining Your Legacy:** Develop strategies to ensure the sustainability and continuity of your legacy.
- **Personal Fulfillment:** Reflect on balancing professional achievements and personal growth in building a legacy.

Creating a lasting legacy is the pinnacle of leadership. Legacy Leadership: Crafting a Lasting Impact will guide you through this transformative journey, helping you to inspire change, empower others, and leave an indelible mark on the world. Prepare to embark on the final chapter of your leadership transformation, focusing on leading with excellence today and ensuring your contributions inspire positive change for future generations.

# WE VALUE YOUR FEEDBACK

Thank you for reading "Resilient Resolve: Overcome Adversity, Maintain Focus, Cultivate Grit, and Build Unstoppable Leadership." Your thoughts and feedback are precious to us and help us improve future editions and other works in the "Leadership Transformed" series.

Please take a moment to share your insights and experiences with this book. Your feedback helps us understand what resonated with you and what can be improved. Here are a few questions to guide your feedback:

- What are your overall impressions of Resilient Resolve?
- Which chapters or sections did you find most useful or impactful?
- How have you applied the concepts of resilience in your leadership role?
- Did you find the writing style engaging and easy to follow?
- Do you have any additional comments or suggestions for improvement?

Leave a review on the platform where you purchased the book. Or you can send your feedback directly to us at mailto:patildilip23@gmail.com

Stay updated with the latest news, resources, and upcoming books in the "Leadership Transformed" series. Join our community and connect with other leaders committed to transforming their leadership practices.

Again, Thank you for your support and for taking the time to provide your feedback. Your insights are invaluable, and we look forward to hearing from you.

With resilience and resolve,

Dilip Patil

# ABOUT THE AUTHOR

Dilip Patil has garnered over thirty years of expertise in the information technology sector, navigating governmental and corporate landscapes where he has been recognized for his professional achievements. Beyond his professional success, Dilip adopts a holistic approach to life, valuing personal growth, well-being, and lifelong learning.

His commitment to maintaining a balance between mind, body, and spirit is exemplified in his role as a devoted yoga instructor and his practice of Ayurvedic life management. These practices underscore his dedication to holistic health and wellness. As an active Toastmasters Club member, he continuously honed his communication and leadership skills, championing the power of effective dialogue and genuine expression.

Born on August 26, 1968, in Pulgaon, a serene village in Maharashtra's Wardha district, Dilip's educational path began at the Hindi-medium Ordinance Factory Higher Secondary School in Katni, Madhya Pradesh. His passion for technology was further nurtured, leading him to earn an Engineering degree from Government Engineering College, Jabalpur, in 1990, followed by a part-time MBA in 2010.

He enjoys a variety of interests, including music, films, motivational literature, and traveling. His dedication to community service, particularly in Nagpur, the vibrant Orange City, highlights his commitment to making a positive societal impact and reflects his belief in transforming challenges into opportunities for growth.

He invites readers to join him on his journey of self-discovery, resilience, and success. Follow him for insights and experiences that light the way to a more fulfilled and intentional life through his social media:

https://www.facebook.com/dilip.patil.3979

https://www.linkedin.com/in/dilip-patil-4066a518

https://www.instagram.com/dilip.patil.3979

Join a community committed to personal development, resilience, and mutual success, fostering an environment of inspiration and continuous growth.

# EXPLORE MORE BOOKS

If you found "Resilient Resolve" valuable, check out the other books in the "**LEADERSHIP TRANSFORMED**" series. Each book delves into critical aspects of modern leadership, offering practical insights and strategies to enhance your leadership skills and drive organizational success.

Through his other esteemed book series, "**THE ART OF SUCCESS**" and "**PROCRASTINATION TRIUMPH**," he delves into varied facets of personal and professional growth. Each series offers a unique perspective on mastering life's challenges and seizing opportunities for success. Discover more of Dilip Patil's work, available across various platforms, and continue your journey of learning and growth.

THE ART OF SUCCESS SERIES

1. Empowering Yourself to Achieve Success: This title empowers you to cultivate a mindset conducive to success and fulfillment. It guides you on a transformative exploration of personal development guided by core principles, actionable strategies, and inspiring anecdotes.

2. The Path to Lasting Happiness: Discover the keys to enduring happiness, navigating aspects like

purpose, mindset, relationships, resilience, and more. Develop communication finesse, nurture empathy, and acquire skills for multifaceted success.

3. Yoga Flow for Tech Minds: This title harmonizes ancient wisdom with modern science to enhance productivity, reduce stress, and foster holistic well-being in the digital age. It offers practices tailored for tech minds seeking balance.

4. The Success Habits: Delve into the psychology of success to instill winning habits and unlock your full potential. Equip yourself with actionable strategies to elevate your productivity, career, and overall fulfillment.

5. The Success Mindset: Discover the secrets to attaining goals and crafting your desired reality. Learn how to nurture a winning mindset, dismantle limiting beliefs, and unleash boundless potential.

6. Endurance: Journey deep into enduring and transcending life's tests—an invaluable companion on your path of growth and adaptability.

7. The Power of Adaptability: This book complements The Success Formula by exploring

adaptability's remarkable influence on shaping destinies.

8. The Success Formula: Unlock success and potential with fundamental principles, tools, and real-life stories. This guide acts as a compass for personal and professional excellence.

9. Discover the Power of Gratitude: Explore the transformative power of gratitude in personal and professional growth.

10. 10 Pillars of Personal Growth: Embrace resilience, Foster Connections, Cultivate Well-being, and Reach the Zenith of Success.

## PROCRASTINATION TRIUMPH SERIES

1. Achieve It Now: An essential guide to overcoming procrastination and improving the future is Beat Procrastination for a Brighter Tomorrow.

2. Temporal Triumph: Defeat Procrastination, Embrace Time Mastery, and Achieve Your Destiny.

3. Action Accelerator: Practical Strategies to Eliminate Procrastination, Propel Your Life and Career Forward.

4. Pathway Pioneer: Overcome Procrastination Through Strategic Habit and Build for Lasting Growth.

1. Leadership Awakening: Ignite Self-Awareness, Build Confidence, Foster Growth, And Embark on Your Leadership Journey

2. Visionary Pathways: Unleash Creativity, Foster Resilience, Amplify Impact, and Master Transformational Leadership

3. Masterful Communication: Enhance Influence, Improve Relationships, Boost Persuasion and Transform Leadership Skills

4. Decision Dynamics: Navigate Complexity, Solve Problems, Cultivate Impact, and Empower Leadership through Strategy

5. Empathy & Empowerment: Connect Deeply, Empower Others, Build Trust, and Create Resonant Leadership

6. Innovative Edge: Foster Creativity, Lead Change, Embrace Challenges, and Shape Modern Leadership

Each book in the series builds on the last, providing a complete arsenal for personal and professional success. To explore these titles further and for purchasing information, please visit https://www.amazon.com/author/patildilip.

# YOUR GIFT: "THE SUCCESS FORMULA"

The Success Formula complements the principles explored in **"Resilient Resolve: Overcome Adversity, Maintain Focus, Cultivate Grit, and Build Unstoppable Leadership"** by providing actionable steps to achieve your goals and enhance your life.

To download your free copy, click the link below or scan the QR code:

This eBook is my way of saying thank you and supporting you in your journey toward success and happiness.

www.ingramcontent.com/pod-product-compliance
Lightning Source LLC
Chambersburg PA
CBHW071932210526
45479CB00002B/652